BOLLINGEN SERIES LXIX

# CHRONIQUE

BY

### ST.-JOHN PERSE, *pseud.*

*Alexis Saint-Léger Léger*

**TRANSLATION BY**
**ROBERT FITZGERALD**

———

*BILINGUAL EDITION*

BOLLINGEN SERIES LXIX
PANTHEON BOOKS

COPYRIGHT © 1961 BY BOLLINGEN FOUNDATION, NEW YORK, N.Y.
PUBLISHED FOR BOLLINGEN FOUNDATION
BY PANTHEON BOOKS INC., NEW YORK, N.Y.
FRENCH TEXT © 1960 BY LIBRAIRIE GALLIMARD, PARIS

THIS VOLUME IS THE SIXTY-NINTH IN A SERIES OF BOOKS
SPONSORED BY AND PUBLISHED FOR
BOLLINGEN FOUNDATION

*Library of Congress Catalogue Card No. 61-9311*
*Manufactured in the United States of America*
*Designed by Bert Clarke*

# CONTENTS

## CHRONIQUE

# CHRONICLE

# CHRONIQUE

# 1

« *G*rand âge, nous voici. Fraîcheur du soir sur les hauteurs, souffle du large sur tous les seuils, et nos fronts mis à nu pour de plus vastes cirques . . .

Un soir de rouge et longue fièvre, où s'abaissent les lances, nous avons vu le ciel en Ouest plus rouge et rose du rose d'insectes des marais salants: soir de grand erg, et très grand orbe, où les premières élisions du jour nous furent telles que défaillances du langage.

Et c'est un déchirement d'entrailles, de viscères, sur toute l'aire illuminée du Siècle: linges lavés dans les eaux mères *et le doigt d'homme promené, au plus violet et vert du ciel, dans ces ruptures ensanglantées du songe — trouées vives!*

*Une seule et lente nuée claire, d'une torsion plus vive par le travers du ciel austral, courbe son ventre blanc de squale aux ailerons de gaze. Et l'étalon rouge du soir hennit dans les calcaires. Et notre songe est en haut lieu. Ascension réglée sur l'ascension des astres, nés de mer . . . Et ce n'est point de même mer que nous rêvons ce soir.*

*Si haut que soit le site, une autre mer au loin s'élève, et qui nous suit, à hauteur du front d'homme: très haute masse et levée d'âge à l'horizon des terres, comme rempart de pierre au front d'Asie, et très haut seuil en flamme à l'horizon des hommes de toujours, vivants et morts de même foule.*

*Lève la tête, homme du soir. La grande rose des ans tourne à ton front serein. Le grand arbre du ciel, comme un nopal, se vêt en Ouest de cochenilles rouges. Et dans l'embrasement d'un soir aux senteurs d'algue sèche, nous éduquons, pour de plus hautes transhumances, de grandes îles à mi-ciel nourries d'arbouses et de genièvre.*

*Fièvre là-haut et lit de braise. Statut d'épouses pour la nuit à toutes cimes lavées d'or!*

# 2

*Grand âge, vous mentiez: route de braise et non de cendres . . . La face ardente et l'âme haute, à quelle outrance encore courons-nous là ? Le temps que l'an mesure n'est point mesure de nos jours. Nous n'avons point commerce avec le moindre ni le pire. Pour nous la turbulence divine à son dernier remous . . .*

*Grand âge, nous voici sur nos routes sans bornes. Claquements du fouet sur tous les cols! Et très haut cri sur la hauteur! Et ce grand vent d'ailleurs à notre encontre, qui courbe l'homme sur la pierre comme l'araire sur la glèbe.*

*Nous vous suivrons, aile du soir . . . Dilatation de l'œil* dans les basaltes et dans les marbres! La voix de l'homme est sur la terre, la main de l'homme est dans la pierre et tire un aigle de sa nuit. Mais Dieu se tait dans le quantième; et notre lit n'est point tiré dans l'étendue ni la durée.

O Mort parée du gantelet d'ivoire, tu croises en vain nos sentes bosselées d'os, car notre route tend plus loin. Le valet d'armes accoutré d'os que nous logeons, et qui nous sert à gages, désertera ce soir au tournant de la route.

Et ceci reste à dire: nous vivons d'outre-mort, et de mort même vivrons-nous. Les chevaux sont passés qui couraient à l'ossuaire, la bouche encore fraîche des sauges de la terre. Et la grenade de Cybèle teint encore de son sang la bouche de nos femmes.

Notre royaume est d'avant-soir, ce grand éclat d'un Siècle vers sa cime; et nous n'y tenons point lits de justice ni camps d'honneur, mais tout un déploiement d'étoffes sur les pentes, déroulant à longs plis ces grands amas de lumière jaune que les Mendiants du soir assemblent de si loin, comme soieries d'Empire et soies grèges de tribut.

Nous en avions assez du doigt de craie sous l'équation sans maître . . . Et vous, nos grands Aînés, dans vos robes rigides, qui descendez les rampes immortelles avec vos *grands livres de pierre, nous avons vu remuer vos lèvres dans la clarté du soir: vous n'avez dit le mot qui lève ni nous suive.*

*Lucine errante sur les grèves pour l'enfantement des œuvres de la femme, il est d'autres naissances à quoi porter vos lampes! . . . Et Dieu l'aveugle luit dans le sel et dans la pierre noire, obsidienne ou granit. Et la roue tourne entre nos mains, comme au tambour de pierre de l'Aztèque.*

# 3

*Grand âge, nous venons de toutes rives de la terre. Notre race est antique, notre face est sans nom. Et le temps en sait long sur tous les hommes que nous fûmes.*

*Nous avons marché seuls sur les routes lointaines; et les mers nous portaient qui nous furent étrangères. Nous avons connu l'ombre et son spectre de jade. Nous avons vu le feu dont s'effaraient nos bêtes. Et le ciel tint courroux dans nos vases de fer.*

*Grand âge, nous voici. Nous n'avions soin de roses ni d'acanthes. Mais la mousson d'Asie fouettait, jusqu'à nos* lits de cuir ou de rotin, son lait d'écume et de chaux vive. De très grands fleuves, nés de l'Ouest, filaient à quatre jours en mer leur chyle épais de limon vert.

Et sur la terre de latérite rouge où courent les cantharides vertes, nous entendions un soir tinter les premières gouttes de pluie tiède, parmi l'envol des rolliers bleus d'Afrique et la descente des grands vols du Nord qui font claquer l'ardoise d'un grand Lac.

Ailleurs des cavaliers sans maîtres échangèrent leurs montures à nos tentes de feutre. Nous avons vu passer l'abeille naine du désert. Et les insectes rouges ponctués de noir s'accouplaient sur le sable des Iles. L'hydre antique des nuits n'a point pour nous séché son sang au feu des villes.

Et nous étions peut-être en mer, ce jour d'éclipse et de première défaillance, quand la louve noire du ciel mordit au cœur le vieil astre de nos pères. Et dans l'abîme gris et vert aux senteurs de semence, couleur de l'œil des nouveaux-nés, nous nous sommes baignés nus — priant, que tout ce bien nous vînt à mal, et tout ce mal à bien.

★

Prédateurs, certes! nous le fûmes; et de nuls maîtres que nous-mêmes tenant nos lettres de franchise — Tant de sanctuaires éventés et de doctrines mises à nu, comme femmes aux hanches découvertes! Enchères aux quais de corail noir, enseignes brûlées sur toutes rades, et nos cœurs au matin comme rades foraines . . .

O vous qui nous meniez à tout ce vif de l'âme, fortune errante sur les eaux, nous direz-vous un soir sur terre quelle main nous vêt de cette tunique ardente de la fable, et de quels fonds d'abîme nous vint à bien, nous vint à mal, toute cette montée d'aube rougissante, et cette part en nous divine qui fut notre part de ténèbres?

Car maintes fois sommes-nous nés, dans l'étendue sans fin du jour. Et qu'est ce mets, sur toutes tables offert, qui nous fut très suspect en l'absence de l'Hôte? Nous passons, et, de nul engendrés, connaît-on bien l'espèce où nous nous avançons? Que savons-nous de l'homme, notre spectre, sous sa cape de laine et son grand feutre d'étranger?

Ainsi l'on voit au soir, dans les gros bourgs de corne où les ruraux prennent leurs semences — toutes fontaines désertées et toute place de boue sèche marquée du piétinement fourchu — les étrangers sans nom ni face, en longue coiffe rabattue, accoster sous l'auvent, contre le montant de pierre de la porte, les grandes filles de la terre fleurant l'ombre et la nuit comme vaisseaux de vin dans l'ombre.

# 4

*Errants, ô Terre, nous rêvions . . .*

*Nous n'avons point tenure de fief ni terre de bien-fonds. Nous n'avons point connu le legs, ni ne saurions léguer. Qui sut jamais notre âge et sut notre nom d'homme? Et qui disputerait un jour de nos lieux de naissance? Éponyme, l'ancêtre, et sa gloire, sans trace. Nos œuvres vivent loin de nous dans leurs vergers d'éclairs. Et nous n'avons de rang parmi les hommes de l'instant.*

*Errants, que savions-nous du lit d'aïeule, tout blasonné qu'il fût dans son bois moucheté des Iles?... Il n'était* point de nom pour nous dans le vieux gong de bronze de l'antique demeure. Il n'était point de nom pour nous dans l'oratoire de nos mères (bois de jacaranda ou de cédrat), ni dans l'antenne d'or mobile au front des gardiennes de couleur.

Nous n'étions pas dans le bois de luthier de l'épinette ou de la harpe; ni dans le col de cygne des grands meubles lustrés, couleur de vin d'épices. Non plus n'étions dans les ciselures du bronze, et dans l'onyx, et les cannelures de pilastres, ni dans les vitres peuplées d'arbres des hautes armoires à livres, tout miel et or et cuir rouge d'Émir,

Mais dans l'écale de tortue géante encore malodorante, et dans le linge des servantes, et dans la cire des selleries où s'égare la guêpe; ah! dans la pierre du vieux fusil de noir, et dans l'odeur de copeaux frais des charpentiers de mer, et dans la guibre du voilier sur chantier de famille; mieux, dans la pâte de corail blanc sciée pour les terrasses, et dans la pierre noire et blanche des grands carrelages d'offices, et dans l'enclume du forgeron d'étable, et dans ce bout de chaîne luisante, sous l'orage, qu'élève, corne haute, la lourde bête noire portant bourse de cuir . . .

L'algue fétide de minuit nous fut compagne sous les combles.

# 5

*Grand âge, nous voici. Rendez-vous pris, et de long-
temps, avec cette heure de grand sens.*

*Le soir descend, et nous ramène, avec nos prises de haute
mer. Nulle dalle familiale où retentisse le pas d'homme.
Nulle demeure à la ville ni cour pavée de roses de pierre
sous les voûtes sonores.*

*Il est temps de brûler nos vieilles coques chargées d'algues.
La Croix du Sud est sur la Douane; la frégate-aigle a
regagné les îles; l'aigle-harpie est dans la jungle, avec le
singe et le serpent-devin. Et l'estuaire est immense sous la
charge du ciel.*

*Grand âge, vois nos prises: vaines sont-elles, et nos mains libres. La course est faite et n'est point faite; la chose est dite et n'est point dite. Et nous rentrons chargés de nuit, sachant de naissance et de mort plus que n'enseigne le songe d'homme. Après l'orgueil, voici l'honneur, et cette clarté de l'âme florissante dans l'épée grande et bleue.*

*Hors des légendes du sommeil toute cette immensité de l'être et ce foisonnement de l'être, toute cette passion d'être et tout ce pouvoir d'être, ah! tout ce très grand souffle voyageur qu'à ses talons soulève, avec l'envol de ses longs plis — très grand profil en marche au carré de nos portes — le passage à grands pas de la Vierge nocturne!*

# 6

...*Comme celui, la main encore au col de sa monture, qui songe au loin et rêve haut: «Je porterai plus loin l'honneur de ma maison» (et la plaine à ses pieds, dans les fumées du soir, roule un guéret très vaste et très bouclé, comme paille de fer, et mesurant le temps boisé du long parcours, il voit — et cela est — tout un là-bas de lointains bleus et d'aigrettes blanches, et la terre au repos paissant ses buffles de légende et ses genévriers),*

*Comme celui, la main tenue sur ses papiers et titres d'acquisition, qui prend mesure d'un grand bien (et l'entrée en jouissance ne comble pas son gré),*

*Nous étendons à tout l'avoir notre usage et nos lois.*

★

*Grand âge, vous régnez . . . L'étage est le plus vaste, et le site si haut que la mer est partout — mer d'outremer et d'outresonge et nourrice d'eaux mères: celle-là même que nous fûmes, et de naissance, en toutes conques marines . . .*

*L'étiage dit son chiffre à hauteur du cœur d'homme, et ce chiffre n'est point chiffre. Et l'Océan des terres, à son étale, pousse ses milliers d'arceaux de mangles et d'arcanes, comme vigne en songe provignée sur l'étendue des eaux.*

*Siffle plus bas, brise d'ailleurs, à la veillée des hommes de grand âge. Notre grief n'est plus de mort. La terre donne son sel. Le soir nous dit un mot de Guèbre. L'esprit des eaux rase le sol comme mouette au désert. Et l'ineffable est sur son aile à hauteur de nos tempes. Il n'est plus mot pour nous que nous n'ayons créé . . .*

*Grand âge, vous régnez, et le silence vous est nombre. Et le songe est immense où se lave le songe. Et l'Océan des choses nous assiège. La mort est au hublot, mais notre route n'est point là. Et nous voici plus haut que songe sur les coraux du Siècle — notre chant.*

Balancement de l'heure, entre toutes choses égales — incréées ou créées... L'arbre illustre sa feuille dans la clarté du soir: le grand arbre Saman qui berce encore notre enfance; ou cet autre, en forêt, qui s'ouvrait à la nuit, élevant à son dieu l'ample charge ouvragée de ses roses géantes.

Grand âge, vous croissez! Rétine ouverte au plus grand cirque; et l'âme avide de son risque... Voici la chose vaste en Ouest, et sa fraîcheur d'abîme sur nos faces.

Ceux qui furent aux choses n'en disent point l'usure ni la cendre, mais ce haut vivre en marche sur la terre des morts... Et la terre fait son bruit de mer au loin sur les coraux, et la vie fait son bruit de ronce en flamme sur les cimes. Et c'est pluie de toujours, au clair-obscur des eaux, de cendre fine et de chaux douce sur les grands fonds soyeux d'abîme sans sommeil.

Jadis des hommes de haut site, la face peinte d'ocre rouge sur leurs mesas d'argile, nous ont dansé sans gestes danse immobile de l'aigle. Ici, ce soir, et face à l'Ouest, mimant la vergue ou le fléau, il n'est que d'étendre les bras en croix pour auner à son aune l'espace d'un tel an: danse immobile de l'âge sur l'envergure de son aile.

Ou bien assis, la main au sol, comme main de pâtre dans

le thym, à tous ces fronts bossués de pierre blanche, nous
affleurons nous-mêmes à tout ce blanc d'amande et de coprah
de la pierre de crête: douceur de spath et de fluor, et beau
lustre du gneiss entre les schistes laminés . . .

Immortelle l'armoise que froisse notre main.

# 7

*Et ramenant enfin les pans d'une plus vaste bure, nous assemblons, de haut, tout ce grand fait terrestre.*

*Derrière nous, par là-bas, au versant de l'année, toute la terre, à plis droits, et de partout tirée, comme l'ample cape de berger jusqu'au menton nouée . . .*

*(Nous faudra-t-il — car l'Océan des choses nous assiège — nous en couvrir le front et le visage, comme l'on voit, au plus haut cap, l'homme de grand songe sous l'orage s'enfouir la tête dans un sac pour converser avec son dieu ?)*

*. . . Et par-dessus l'épaule, jusqu'à nous, nous entendons ce ruissellement en cours de toute la chose hors des eaux.*

*C'est la terre, de partout, tissant sa laine fauve comme byssus de mer; et le cheminement, à fond de plaines, de ces grandes ombres bleu de Mai qui mènent en silence la transhumance du ciel sur terre . . .*

*Irréprochable, ô terre, ta chronique, au regard du Censeur! Nous sommes pâtres du futur, et ce n'est pas assez pour nous de toute l'immense nuit dévonienne pour étayer notre louange . . . Sommes-nous, ah, sommes-nous bien? — ou fûmes-nous jamais — dans tout cela?*

★

*. . . Et tout cela nous vint à bien, nous vint à mal: la terre mouvante dans son âge et son très haut langage — plissements en cours et charriages, déportements en Ouest et dévoiements sans fin, et sur ses nappes étagées comme barres d'estuaires et déferlements de mer, l'incessante avancée de sa lèvre d'argile . . .*

*O face insigne de la Terre, qu'un cri pour toi se fasse entendre, dernière venue dans nos louanges! L'amour durcit tes baies sauvages, ô terre plus crépelée que le chagrin des Maures! ô mémoire, au cœur d'homme, du royaume perdu!*

*Le Ciel en Ouest se vêt comme un Khalife, la terre lave*

20

ses vignes au rouge de bauxite, et l'homme se lave au vin de nuit: le tonnelier devant son chai, le forgeron devant sa forge, et le roulier penché sur l'auge de pierre des fontaines.

Honneur aux vasques où nous buvons! Les tanneries sont lieu d'offrande et les chiens s'ensanglantent aux déchets de boucherie; mais pour le songe de nos nuits, les démascleurs de chênes ont mis à jour un ton plus riche et grave, couleur tête de maure.

... O mémoire, prends souci de tes roses de sel. La grande rose du soir héberge l'étoile sur son sein comme une cétoine dorée. Hors des légendes du sommeil ce nantissement de l'homme chargé d'astres!

Grand âge, vous louez. Les femmes se lèvent dans la plaine et marchent à grands pas au cuivre rouge de l'existence.

La horde des Siècles a passé là!

# 8

...*Grand âge, nous voici — et nos pas d'hommes vers l'issue. C'est assez d'engranger, il est temps d'éventer et d'honorer notre aire.*

*Demain, les grands orages maraudeurs, et l'éclair au travail . . . Le caducée du ciel descend marquer la terre de son chiffre. L'alliance est fondée.*

*Ah! qu'une élite aussi se lève, de très grands arbres sur la terre, comme tribu de grandes âmes et qui nous tiennent en leur conseil . . . Et la sévérité du soir descende, avec l'aveu de sa douceur, sur les chemins de pierre brûlante éclairés de lavande . . .*

Frémissement alors, à la plus haute tige engluée d'ambre, de la plus haute feuille mi-déliée sur son onglet d'ivoire.

Et nos actes s'éloignent dans leurs vergers d'éclairs . . .

A d'autres d'édifier, parmi les schistes et les laves. A d'autres de lever les marbres à la ville.

Pour nous chante déjà plus hautaine aventure. Route frayée de main nouvelle, et feux portés de cime en cime . . .

Et ce ne sont point là chansons de toile pour gynécée, ni chansons de veillée, dites chansons de Reine de Hongrie, pour égréner le maïs rouge au fil rouillé des vieilles rapières de famille,

Mais chant plus grave, et d'autre glaive, comme chant d'honneur et de grand âge, et chant du Maître, seul au soir, à se frayer sa route devant l'âtre

— fierté de l'âme devant l'âme et fierté d'âme grandissante dans l'épée grande et bleue.

Et nos pensées déjà se lèvent dans la nuit comme les hommes de grande tente, avant le jour, qui marchent au ciel rouge portant leur selle sur l'épaule gauche.

Voici les lieux que nous laissons. Les fruits du sol sont sous nos murs, les eaux du ciel dans nos citernes, et les grandes meules de porphyre reposent sur le sable.

L'offrande, ô nuit, où la porter ? et la louange, la fier ? . . . Nous élevons à bout de bras, sur le plat de nos mains, comme couvée d'ailes naissantes, ce cœur enténébré de l'homme où fut l'avide, et fut l'ardent, et tant d'amour irrévélé . . .

Écoute, ô nuit, dans les préaux déserts et sous les arches solitaires, parmi les ruines saintes et l'émiettement des vieilles termitières, le grand pas souverain de l'âme sans tanière,

Comme aux dalles de bronze où rôderait un fauve.

★

Grand âge, nous voici. Prenez mesure du cœur d'homme.»

Septembre 1959

24

# CHRONICLE

# 1

" Great age, behold us. Coolness of evening on the heights,
breath of the open sea on every threshold, and our foreheads
bared for wider spaces . . .

An evening of crimson and long fever where lances incline
and lengthen, we have seen the sky to Westward redder and
deeper rose, the rose of sea-larvae from the salt marshes:
evening of vast Saharan space, and ever-widening sky,
where the first lapses of the light seemed to us like failures of
language.

And there is a rending of entrails, of viscera, over the
whole lighted space of the Century: linens laved in primaeval

waters and the finger of man probing, in the sky's deepest violet and green, those bleeding ruptures of dream — live wounds!

One lingering pale cloud across the austral sky, in living torsion yonder, bends a white shark-belly with gauzy fins. And the red stallion of evening neighs in the red clays. And our dream is on the heights. Ascension timed by the rising of stars, born of the sea . . . And it is not of that sea that we dream this evening.

High though the site may be, another sea rises far away and is level with us, at the height of man's forehead: a very high mass and uprising of the ages at the horizon of earth, like a rampart of stone on the brow of Asia, and a very high threshold aflame at the horizon of men the everlasting, living and dead in one crowd.

Raise your head, man of evening. The great rose of the years turns round your serene brow. The great tree of the sky, like a nopal, robes itself in the West with scarlet flies, cochineal. And in the fiery glow of an evening fragrant with dry seaweed, we lead toward higher pasturings great islands in mid-sky, robust with bushes of arbutus and juniper.

Fever on the heights and bed of glowing embers. Statute of brides for a night to all summits washed in gold!

# 2

Great age, you lied: a road of glowing embers, not of ash . . . With face alight and spirit high, to what extreme are we still running? Time measured by the year is no measure of our days. We hold no traffic with the least nor with the worst. Divine turbulence be ours to its last eddy . . .

Great age, behold us on our limitless ways. Cracking of whips on all the passes! And a loud cry on the height! And this great wind from elsewhere meeting us, a wind that bends man over the rock like the ploughman over the glebe.

We will follow you, wing of evening . . . Dilation of the eye within rocks of basalt and marble! The voice of man is upon the earth, his hand is in the rock and draws an eagle from its night. But God does not dwell in the date or day; and our bed is not laid in place or time.

O Death adorned with ivory gauntlet, you cross in vain our paths cobbled with bones, for our way lies beyond. The squire-at-arms accoutred in bones, whom we house and who serves for a wage, will desert this evening at the bend in the road.

And this remains to be said: we live on what is beyond death, and on death itself shall we live. The horses running to the ossuary have passed by, with mouths yet freshened by the cool sage of the meadow. And the pomegranate of Cybele still stains with its blood the mouths of our women.

Our kingdom is of the hour before night, this great flame of a Century toward its crest; and here we hold no beds of justice or fields of honour, but everywhere an opening and display of fabrics on the slopes, rolling out in long folds those masses of yellow light that Mendicants of evening gather in from so far away, like silken stuffs of Empire and raw silks of tribute.

We had had enough of the finger of chalk beneath the un-taught equation . . . And you, our great Elders, in your rigid robes, descending the immortal ramps with your massive books of stone, we have seen your lips tremble in the clear light of evening: but you spoke not the word that would live and be with us.

Lucina wandering at night on all shores of the earth in search of women in labour, there are other births worthy of your lamps! . . . And God the blind glitters in the salt and the black rock, obsidian or granite. And the wheel turns between our hands, as on the stone drum of the Aztec.

# 3

Great age, we come from all the shores of the earth. Our race is ancient, our face is nameless. And time has long known more than it tells of all the men we were.

We have walked the distant roads alone; and seas have borne us that to us were strangers. We have known the shade and his jade spectre. We have seen the fire that cast fear among our beasts. And heaven's wrath forked in our jars of iron.

Great age, behold us. We cherished neither rose nor acanthus. But the monsoon of Asia drove into our beds of rawhide or rattan, lashing its milk of foam and quicklime.

Giant rivers, born of the West, carried four days out to sea their heavy chyle of green silt.

And on the earth of red laterite where the green cantharides run, we heard one evening the first drops of warm rain ringing, amid the rising clouds of blue rollers of Africa and the descent of great flights from the North, beating on the slate of a great Lake.

In other lands, horsemen who knew no master have changed their mounts at our tents of felt. We have seen the dwarf bee of the desert passing by. And red insects punctuated with black coupling on the sand of the Islands. The ancient hydra of the nights has not dried its blood for us at the fire of cities.

And we were at sea perhaps, that day of eclipse and first defection, when the black she-wolf of the sky bit to the heart the ancient star of our fathers. And in the grey-green abyss with its odour of semen, colour of newborn infants' eyes, we bathed naked — praying that for us all this good come to ill, and all this ill to good.

★

Plunderers, indeed! we were; and carrying letters of marque from no masters but ourselves. — So many sanc-

*33*

tuaries laid open to the wind, so many doctrines laid bare, like women whose thighs were uncovered! Crying of auction along quays of black coral, ensigns burned over every harbour, and our hearts at morning like open roadsteads . . .

O you who led us to all this quick of the soul, fortune wandering on the waters, will you tell us one evening on earth what hand arrays us in this burning tunic of fable, and from what abysmal depth, for our good, for our ill, came all that welling of reddening dawn, and that divine part in us that was our part of darkness?

For many times were we born, in the endless reach of day. And what is that repast, offered on every table, that we found so suspect in the absence of the Host? We pass, and, engendered of no one, do we really know toward what species we are advancing? What do we know of man, our spectre, under his woolen cape and his stranger's broad hat?

Thus one sees, at evening, in cattle-towns where country-men buy their seed — all the fountains deserted and on every square dry mud tracked by cloven hooves — those strangers without names or faces, their tall headgear pulled down, stopping under the eaves to accost the big country girls who lean against door jambs, smelling of dusk and night like a jar of wine in the shade.

34

# 4

Wandering, O Earth, we dreamed . . .

No holdings have we in fee, no landed property. We have known no legacy, nor could we make any. Who has ever known our age, known our name as man? And who would ever dispute the place of our birth? Eponymous is our ancestor, and his glory without trace. Our works live far from us in their orchards of lightning. And we hold no rank among men of the moment.

Wandering, what did we know of our ancestral bed, all blazoned though it were in that speckled wood of the Islands? . . . There was no name for us in the ancient bronze gong of the old family house. There was no name for us in our mothers' oratory (jacaranda wood or cedar), nor in the golden antennae quivering in the head-dresses of our guardians, women of colour.

We were not in the lute-maker's wood, in the spinet or the harp; nor in the polished swans' necks of great pieces of furniture, colour of spiced wine. Nor were we in the chasings of bronzes, nor in the onyx; not in the flutings of pilasters, nor in the glass fronts, peopled with trees, of the tall book-cases, all honey and gold and red leather of an Emir,

But in the shell of the giant tortoise, malodorous still, and in the linens of the serving women, and in the wax of the harness-rooms where the wasp has strayed; ah! in the flint of the black man's old flintlock, and in the fresh chip odour of the ship's carpenter, and in the bow of the sailing craft on the family launching ways; better still, in the block of white coral sawn for the terraces, and in the black and white of the great floor tiles in the pantry, and in the anvil of the stable forge, and in that length of chain glinting under a thunderstorm when the heavy black beast, swinging his leather pouch, rears with horns tossed high . . .

The fetid seaweed of midnight was with us under the gables.

# 5

Great age, behold us. Rendezvous accepted, and long ago, with this hour of deep meaning.

The evening descends, and brings us back, with our catch from the high seas. No family flagstone rings with our stride. No great house in the city, nor courtyard paved with rose-patterned stones, under the echoing arches.

It is time to burn our old hulks laden with algae. The Southern Cross is over the Custom-house; the frigate-bird has regained the islands; the harpy-eagle is in the jungle, with the monkey and the wizard-snake. And the estuary is immense under the load of sky.

Great age, see our takings: vain they are, and our hands free. The voyage is made and not made; the thing is said and not said. And we come back laden with night, knowing of birth and death more than man's dream can teach. After pride, behold honour, and that clarity of the soul that flourishes in the great blue sword.

Outside the legends of sleep all that immensity of being and profusion of being, all that passion of being and power of being, ah! all that great voyaging wind that the wandering Goddess raises at her heels, in the flight of her long folds, as she passes with long strides in the night — a towering profile in the frame of our doorways!

# 6

Like one, his hand still resting on the neck of his mount, who ponders afar and dreams high: 'I shall carry still farther the honour of my house' (and the plain at his feet, under the fumes of evening, rolls out a vast ploughland, tight-curled like steel wool, and measuring the timbered span of the long faring he sees — and it is there — a prospect all of blue distance and white plumes, and the earth at rest pasturing its legendary buffaloes and its juniper-trees),

Like one, his hand firm on his papers and titles of ownership, who takes the measure of a great estate (and entering upon its enjoyment does not bring him peace),

We extend to all possession our usage and our laws.

★

Great age, you reign . . . The stage is the widest, and the site so high that the sea is everywhere — sea beyond seas and dreams and nurse of primaeval waters: that very one which we were, and from birth, in all the conch-shells of the sea . . .

The tide tells its height at the height of man's heart, and this measure is no measure. And the Ocean of lands, at flood-tide, curves out in thousands its arches of mangrove and mystery, like a vine in dream relayed over the expanding waters.

Whistle more softly, breeze from afar, in the vigil of men of great age. Our grievance is no longer against death. Earth gives its salt. The evening speaks as a Gheber, worshipper of fire. The spirit of the waters goes skimming the soil like a gull in the desert. And the ineffable is on its wing at the height of our foreheads. There is no word now for us that we do not create . . .

Great age, you reign, and the silence for you is number. And the dream is immense there where the dream bathes.

And the Ocean of things lays siege to us. Death is at the porthole, but our course does not lie that way. And behold us higher than dream on the corals of the Century — our song.

Equipoise of the hour, between all things equal — increate or created . . . The tree glorifies its leaf in the clarity of evening: the great Saman tree that still cradles our childhood; or that other, in the forest, that spread itself open to the night, raising to its god the ample and finely wrought burden of its giant roses.

Great age, growing greater! Retina wide open on the circuit of greatest range; and the soul avid for the soul's risk . . . Behold the vastness in the West, and cool from the abyss its freshness on our faces.

Those who were in the midst of things do not speak of waste and ashes but of this high moment in living, moving over the earth of the dead . . . And the earth makes its sound of sea far off on the corals, and life makes its sound of thorn-fires on the crests. And there is in the light and shade of deep waters an everlasting rain of fine ash and soft lime sifting down on the silken bed of the living deep-sea floor.

Long ago men of the highland, on their clay mesas, with

faces painted in red ochre, danced for us without gestures the motionless dance of the eagle. Here, this evening, with face to the West, miming the yard-arm or the cross-bar, one has only to stretch one's arms out to span at one's own span the space of a year such as that: motionless dance of age on the spread of its wing.

Or seated, one hand on the ground, like a herdsman's hand in thyme, amid all these jutting foreheads of white stone, we too emerge in all this almond-white and copra-white stone of the crest: smoothness of spar and fluorspar, and fine lustre of gneiss through the laminated schist . . .

Immortal the wild sage that our hand crushes.

# 7

And thus, high seated, gathering at last the pieces of a wider fabric, we assemble around us all this great terrestrial fact.

Behind us, down there on the slope of the year, the whole earth in straight folds and from all sides drawn in, like the ample cloak of a shepherd knotted up to the chin . . .

(Must we — for the Ocean of things lays siege to us — cover forehead and face? As on the highest headland, under the storm, the man of a great dream may be seen burying his head in a sack to converse with his god?)

. . . And over our shoulder, from this summit, we hear the incessant dripping of the whole world new risen out of the waters.

It is the earth, on all sides, weaving its tawny wool like hemp of byssus from the sea; and the procession, on the far plains, of those great May-blue shadows that lead the herds of heaven so silently over the earth . . .

Irreproachable your chronicle, O earth, to the Censor's eye! We are herdsmen of the future, and all the great Devonian night does not suffice to sustain our praise . . . Are we, ah, are we? — or were we ever — in all that?

★

. . . And all that came to us for good, came to us for ill: the earth moving in its age and its lofty idiom — formation of folds and overfolds, displacements toward the West and endless shifting of watercourses, and on tiered layers like sand-bars at tide-mouth, like unfurlings of surf, the incessant advance of a lip of clay . . .

O memorable face of the Earth, let a cry be heard for you, last come in our praises! Love hardened your wild berries,

O earth more wrinkled than sorrow of the Moors! O memory, in man's heart, of the lost kingdom!

The Sky to Westward robes itself like a Caliph, the earth bathes its vines in the red of bauxite, and man bathes in the wine of night: the cooper before his casks, the smith before his forge, and the waggoner bent over the stone trough of the fountains.

Honour to the basins where we drink! The tanneries are places of offering and dogs are smeared with blood from the butcher's waste; but for the dream of our nights, the cutters of bark from the cork-tree have bared a richer tone and darker, colour of a Moor's head.

. . . O memory, take thought for your roses of salt. The great rose of evening lodges a star on its breast like a golden beetle. Beyond the legends of sleep, this pledge to man under his burden of stars!

Great age, you form this praise. The women rise on the plain and march with long steps toward the red copper of existence.

This way has passed the horde of Centuries!

# 8

...Great age, behold us — and our mortal strides toward the issue. Enough of garnering, it is time to air the harvest and honour the threshing floor.

Tomorrow, the great raiding thunderstorms, and the lightning at work . . . The caduceus of the sky descends to mark the earth with its sign. The alliance is sealed.

Ah! may an *élite* also rise, of very tall trees on the earth, like a tribe of great souls that shall hold us of their council . . . And let the severity of evening descend, with avowal of its tenderness, on the roads of burning stone, roads lit with lavender . . .

A quivering then, on the highest stem sticky with amber, of the highest leaf half-detached on its ivory claw.

And our actions dwindle far off in their orchards of lightning . . .

It is for others to build, amid the schist and the lava. For others to raise the marbles in the city.

For us, already, a song of higher adventure. The road traced by a new hand, and fires carried from crest to crest . . .

And these are no weaving songs for the women's quarters, nor fireside songs like 'Queen of Hungary songs' for the shucking of red corn on the rusted blades of old family rapiers,

But a graver song, of another steel, like a song of honour and great age and a song of the Master, alone in the evening, forging his way, before the hearthfire

— pride of the soul before the soul and pride of soul growing to greatness in the great blue sword.

Already our thoughts rise in the night like nomad chieftains of the big tents who walk before daybreak toward a red sky, carrying their saddles on their left shoulders.

Behold the places we leave. The fruits of the soil are beneath our walls, the waters of the sky in our cisterns, and the great millstones of porphyry rest on the sand.

The offering, O night, where to bring it? and the praise, to whom entrust it? . . . We raise, with arms outstretched, on the flat of our hands, like a hatching of nascent wings, this darkened heart of a man where hunger was, and ardour, and so much love unrevealed . . .

Listen, O night, in the deserted courtyards and under the solitary arches, amid the holy ruins and the crumbling of old termite hills, hear the great sovereign footfalls of the soul without a lair,

Like a wild beast prowling a pavement of bronze.

★

Great age, behold us. Take the measure of man's heart."

*September 1959*

# BIBLIOGRAPHY

# I

## CHRONIQUE

### IN FRENCH

*Chronique* was first published in the *Cahiers du Sud* (Marseilles), XLVIII: 352 (October–November 1959). Of that impression, an offprint, with separate pagination, a specially printed cover, and the author's portrait, was issued at Marseilles, October 1960, in some one hundred numbered copies, for private distribution.

First edition: a volume in large format ("jésus" quarto, 28×28 cm.), and large typography (Garamond italics), in a run limited to fifteen numbered copies on "Japon impérial" and one hundred numbered copies on Dutch vellum, was issued by N. R. F., Gallimard, Paris, 1960. Regular edition, in large format, by N. R. F., Gallimard, 1960.

### IN SWEDISH

*Krönika*, bilingual edition with translation by Dag Hammarskjöld facing the French text, was published by Albert Bonniers Forlag, Stockholm, 1960.

### IN GERMAN

*Chronik*, the translation by Friedhelm Kemp, was first published in the review *Merkur* (Stuttgart), 1 November 1960; afterwards as a book, in a bilingual edition, with French text facing, Luchterhand Verlag, Darmstadt, Berlin, and Neuwied, 1960.

IN ENGLISH

*Chronique*, the translation by Robert Fitzgerald, was first published in the review *Encounter* (London), XVI: 2 (February 1961); afterwards as a book, in a bilingual edition, the English version (*Chronicle*) following the French text, as Bollingen Series LXIX, Pantheon Books, New York, 1961.

IN HINDI, ETC.

*Chronique*, in Oriya, Bengali, and Hindi translations by Prafulla Chandra Das, planned for publication by Manmohan House, Cuttack (Orissa), 1961.

IN SPANISH

*Crónica*, translation by Manuel Alvarez Ortega, published in the review *Poesía Española* (Madrid), "Número especial dedicado a Saint-John Perse" (No. 95), November 1960.

*Crónica*, translation by Lysandro Z. D. Galtier, in preparation for publication as a book by Compañía General Fabril Editora, Buenos Aires, 1961.

IN ITALIAN

*Crònaca*, translation in preparation by Romeo Lucchese, for publication as a book, by Lerici Editori, Milan, 1961.

# II

## OTHER WORKS OF ST.-JOHN PERSE

*Published as Books, in French and in Translation*

### ÉLOGES (and Other Poems)

IN FRENCH

Paris, N. R. F., Marcel Rivière, 1911 (signed "Saintléger Léger").

Second edition: Paris, N. R. F., Gallimard, 1925 (revised, signed "St.-J. Perse"; including *Amitié du Prince* and *Chanson du Présomptif*).

Third edition: Paris, N. R. F., Gallimard, 1948 (revised, enlarged, and rearranged; including *Berceuse*).

London, Chester Editions, 1922: *Images à Crusoé: Sept Poèmes d'Éloges*, set to music by Louis Durey.

Paris, Durand, 1923: *Éloges: Poème V*, set to music by Darius Milhaud.

Paris, Ronald Davis, 1924: *Amitié du Prince*. With facsimile of the manuscript.

Milan (Italy), Vanni Schweiwiller, 1959: *Amitié du Prince*.

IN SPANISH

Buenos Aires, Proa, 1925: *Para Festejar una Infancia*. Translation by Ricardo Guiraldes.

Mexico City, Costa-Amic, 1946: *Elogios y otros Poemas*. Translation by Jorge Zalamea.

IN GERMAN

Berlin, Karl-Heinz Henssel Verlag, 1952: *Preislieder*. Translation by Rudolf Kassner and Herbert Steiner. (Publication suspended. Published in *Das Lot*, No. 6, Berlin, 1952.)

IN ENGLISH

New York, W. W. Norton and Co., 1944: *Éloges and Other Poems*. French text facing translation by Louise Varèse, with introduction by Archibald MacLeish.

New York, Bollingen Series, Pantheon Books, 1956: *Éloges and Other Poems*. French text facing a revised translation by Louise Varèse, with an additional poem *Berceuse* and without introduction. (Reprinted 1960.)

ANABASE

IN FRENCH

Paris, N. R. F., Gallimard, 1924; second edition, 1925; third edition, 1947; fourth edition, 1948 (revised and corrected).

New York, Brentano's, 1945.

IN ENGLISH

London, Faber and Faber, Ltd., 1930: *Anabasis*. French text facing translation by T. S. Eliot, with preface by T. S. Eliot. Second edition, 1959: revised and corrected, with bibliography, and notes by Valery Larbaud, Hugo von Hofmannsthal, Giuseppe Ungaretti, and Lucien Fabre.

*54*

New York, Harcourt, Brace and Co., 1938: *Anabasis*. French text with translation and preface by T. S. Eliot. Translation revised and corrected by T. S. Eliot for this edition. Second edition, 1949: translation again revised and corrected by T. S. Eliot.

## IN RUSSIAN

Paris, J. Povolovsky, 1926: *Anabasis*. Translation by G. Adamovitch and G. Ivanoff, with preface by Valery Larbaud.

## IN GERMAN

Leipzig, Insel Verlag, 1929: *Anabasis*. Translation by Bernard Groethuysen and Walter Benjamin, with preface by Hugo von Hofmannsthal. (Publication suspended. Published in *Das Lot*, No. 4, Berlin, 1950.)

Bühl (Baden), Roland-Verlag, 1948: *Anabasis*. French text with translation and introductory note by Kurt Wais. (Publication suspended.)

## IN SPANISH

Mexico City, Contemporáneos, 1931: *Anabasis*. French text with translation and preface by Octavio J. Barreda.

Mexico City, Letras de Mexico, 1940: French text with translation and preface by Octavio J. Barreda.

Bogotá, Universidad Nacional de Colombia, 1950: *Anabasis*. Translation and introduction by Jorge Zalamea.

Madrid, Ediciones Rialp (Adonais), 1957: *Anabasis*. Translation, prologue, and notes by Agustín Larrauri.

## IN ROMANIAN

Bucharest, Cartea Romaneasca, 1932: *Anabasis*. Translation and preface by Ion Pillat.

IN ITALIAN

Rome, Edizione di Novissima, 1936: *Anabasis*. Translation and preface by Giuseppe Ungaretti.


IN SWEDISH

Stockholm, Bonnier, 1939: *Anabasis*. Translation by Arthur Lundkvist, in his *Ikarus Flygt*.


IN GREEK

Athens, Collection de l'Institut Français d'Athènes, 1957: ΑΝΑΒΑΣΗ. Translation and preface by Takis Papatzonis.


IN DANISH

Copenhagen, Gyldendal, 1960: *Anabasis og Eksil*. Translation and preface by Thorkild Hansen.


IN SERBIAN

Belgrade, M. A. B., 1960: *Ahabaca*. Translation and preface by Nikolas Tzaikovitch.


IN HINDI, ETC.

Cuttack (Orissa), Manmohan House, 1961: *Anabasis*. Oriya, Bengali, and Hindi translations by Prafulla Chandra Das.


IN FINNISH

Helsinki, Kustannusosakeyhtio Otava, 1961. *Anabasis*. (Translation in preparation.)

# EXIL

## (with *Poème à l'Étrangère, Pluies, Neiges*)

IN FRENCH

Buenos Aires, Éditions des "Lettres Françaises," 1942: *Exil.*

Neuchâtel (Switzerland), Éditions de la Baconnière, 1942: *Exil.*

Marseilles, Cahiers du Sud, 1942: *Exil.*

"En France," 1942: *Exil.* A clandestine and very limited edition, by Gallimard.

Buenos Aires, Éditions des "Lettres Françaises," 1943: *Pluies.*

Buenos Aires, Éditions des "Lettres Françaises," 1944: *Quatre poèmes 1941–1944* (including *Exil, Poème à l'Étrangère, Pluies, Neiges*); second edition, 1945.

Paris, N. R. F., Gallimard, 1945: *Exil, suivi de Poème à l'Étrangère, Pluies, Neiges*; second edition, 1946 (revised and corrected).

IN SPANISH

Milan (Italy), Italgeo, 1946: *Lluvias, Nieves, Exilio.* Translation by Jorge Zalamea, illustrations by Luni.

IN ENGLISH

New York, Bollingen Series, Pantheon Books, 1949: *Exile and Other Poems.* French text with translation by Denis Devlin and notes by Archibald MacLeish, Roger Caillois, and Alain Bosquet, and bibliography. Second edition, 1953: French text facing the aforementioned translation, without notes, in smaller format. (Reprinted 1961.)

IN GERMAN

Berlin, Karl-Heinz Henssel Verlag, 1949: *Exil, Gedicht an eine Fremde, Regen, Schnee*. Translation by L. Ringelnatz and Wolfgang Rüttenauer.

Frankfurt a.M., Insel-Verlag, 1961 (Insel Bücherei, 730): *Exil*. Translation by Leonharda Gescher and Friedhelm Kemp.

IN DANISH

Copenhagen, Gyldendal, 1960: *Anabasis og Exsil*. Translation and preface by Thorkild Hansen.

IN DUTCH

The Hague, Firma L. J. C. Boucher, 1961: *Anabasis*. Translation by F. C. Terborgh.

IN JAPANESE

Tokyo, Heibon-Sha Editions. (Translation in preparation.)

## VENTS

IN FRENCH

Paris, N. R. F., Gallimard, 1946.

IN ENGLISH

New York, Bollingen Series, Pantheon Books, 1953: *Winds*. French text with translation by Hugh Chisholm, notes by Paul Claudel, Gaëton Picon, Albert Bèguin, and Gabriel Bounoure, and bibliography. Second edition,

1961: French text facing the aforementioned translation, without notes, in smaller format.

## AMERS

IN FRENCH

Paris, N. R. F., Gallimard, 1957.

IN ENGLISH

New York, Bollingen Series, Pantheon Books, 1958: *Seamarks*. French text with translation by Wallace Fowlie, and bibliography. Second edition, 1958: French text facing the aforementioned translation, in smaller format. (Reprinted 1961.)

IN GERMAN

Darmstadt, Berlin, and Neuwied, Hermann Luchterhand Verlag, 1958: *See-Marken*. French text facing translation by Friedhelm Kemp, with a commentary and a letter by St.-John Perse.

IN SPANISH

Buenos Aires, Ediciones Sur. (Translation in preparation.)

## COLLECTED VOLUMES

IN FRENCH

Paris, N. R. F., Gallimard, 1953: *Œuvre poétique* I. Including *Éloges*, *La Gloire des Rois*, *Anabase*, *Exil*, *Vents*. Second edition, 1960: *Œuvre poétique*

I (including *Éloges*, *La Gloire des Rois*, *Anabase*, *Exil*) and II (including *Vents*, *Amers*, *Chronique*).

IN SWEDISH

Stockholm, Bonnier, 1956: *Saint-John Perse: Jord, Vindar, Hav.* Translation and introduction by Erik Lindegren. (Including selections from *Éloges*, *Anabase*, *Exil*, *Vents*, and *Amers*.)


IN GERMAN

Darmstadt, Berlin, and Neuwied, Hermann Luchterhand Verlag, 1957, 1959: (Vol. I) *Saint-John Perse: Dichtungen.* French text facing translation by Friedhelm Kemp, with commentaries and notes by Valery Larbaud, Hugo von Hofmannsthal, T. S. Eliot, Paul Claudel, Alain Bosquet, and Friedhelm Kemp, and bibliography. (Vol. II) *Saint-John Perse: See-Marken.* French text facing translation by Friedhelm Kemp, with a commentary and a letter by St.-John Perse.


IN SPANISH

Buenos Aires, Compañía General Fabril Editora, 1960: *Antología poética de Saint-John Perse.* Selection translated with prologue by Jorge Zalamea.


IN ITALIAN

Milan, Lerici Editori, 1960: *Opere poetiche di Saint-John Perse.* Translations by Giuseppe Ungaretti and Romeo Lucchese. A complete edition in two volumes.